Nature
Spotting Guide

Illustrated by
Stephanie Fizer Coleman

Words by Sam Smith
and Kirsteen Robson

Designed by Jenny Addison

Using this book

You can browse through this book to find out what animals, flowers and trees you might see in a garden, park or wood.

When you spot something outside, see if you can match it to a picture to find out more about it.

Contents

Birds
4-23

Trees
24-43

Bugs
44-65

Flowers
66-85

Other animals
86-93

Index
94-96

Garden birds

Goldfinch

These bright birds have a bouncy flight and a twittering song. They feed in flocks on small seeds.

Look for the yellow bar on its wings

Female is light brown

Bullfinch

Found in thick hedges and on the edges of woods. Its call is a soft 'pee-ew'.

Male has a bright orange chest

This is a male – females are light brown all over

Chaffinch

The rhythm of its song sounds like, 'Sweet, sweet, sweet. Pretty lovey, meet me here'.

Greenfinch

Easiest to spot in winter. In spring, it calls with a wheezy 'dweep' sound.

Blue tit

Watch for flocks of these blue-and-yellow birds darting around feeders in winter.

Young birds have paler feathers

Broad black band on its chest

Great tit

Look out for it in woodlands and gardens. Its song sounds like 'tea-cher tea-cher'.

Garden birds

Song thrush

Listen out for its warbling song. It's often seen breaking open snail shells on rocks.

Its pale chest is speckled with darker spots

Dunnock

Watch for these shy birds feeding on the ground under bird tables, shrubs and hedges.

Flicks its wings as it walks

Robin

Robins sing cheerfully all year round, even on chilly winter days. Their alarm call is 'tic-tic-tic'.

A male blackbird (females are brown)

Blackbird

You'll often hear male blackbirds singing their loud, musical song at sunrise or sunset.

Wren

A very small bird with a surprisingly loud song. It scurries around like a mouse, never staying still for long.

Often holds its tail upright like this

Spot the dark ring around its neck

Collared dove

This dove perches in large gardens, parks or near farm buildings, repeating its gentle 'coo-coooo-coo' call.

Town birds

Feral pigeon

Very easy to spot in towns and cities, pecking at scraps on the pavement. They nest on ledges and shop signs.

Can be black, grey, white, or a mixture

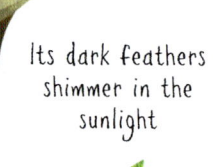

Its dark feathers shimmer in the sunlight

Starling

Often flies in huge, swirling flocks at dusk. It mimics the songs of other birds, and sounds such as phones or car alarms.

House sparrow

Look out for sparrows wherever there are people. They live in flocks, calling to each other with a noisy 'cheep cheep'.

This is a male – females are brown all over

Magpie

Found everywhere from parks and gardens to woods and fields, magpies have a loud 'chacker-chacker' call.

Long tail is very noticeable in flight

Swift

Listen for swifts' screaming calls on summer evenings. They fly fast, often in flocks, catching insects.

Short tail is forked

Pied wagtail

Wags its tail as it walks and bobs up and down as it flies. Its call is a cheery 'chi-zick'.

Runs along on pavements and car parks

Woodland birds

Jay

This shy bird often hides in trees and sometimes visits gardens. Its call is a harsh 'skairk, skairk'.

Look for its white bottom in flight

Blackcap

Moves from perch to perch singing its chattering song. Its alarm call sounds like pebbles tapping together.

Female's cap is brown

Some fly to north Africa for the winter

Spends the winter in southern Africa

Willow warbler

Seen in summer. Its pale legs and high-to-low song help to tell it apart from a chiffchaff.

Woodland birds

Nests in tree-holes

Nuthatch

This short-tailed bird climbs up and down trees in a series of short hops, hunting insects.

Coal tit

Likes conifer woods, where it eats seeds from fir cones, but you might also spot one in a park or garden.

Flies in flocks with other tits in winter

Long-tailed tit

Look for groups of these little birds in hedgerows and at the edges of woods, calling 'see see see' to each other.

Its tail is longer than its body

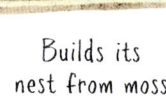

Builds its nest from moss

Grey feathers on the back of its head

Jackdaw

They often nest in big groups, near old trees, old buildings, or cliffs – listen for them cawing and cackling noisily.

Carrion crow

More often seen alone or in pairs, pecking at dead animals or food left on the ground. It has a deep, harsh 'kraa-kraa' call.

Glossy black feathers

Treecreeper

This bird's mottled brown feathers help it to blend in as it climbs up tree trunks, searching for food.

Strong claws for gripping tree bark

Farmland birds

House martin

Seen in summer. They use mud to build cup-shaped nests under the edges of roofs.

Catches insects in flight

Forked tail is shorter than a swallow's

Swallow

Look for these summer visitors twisting and turning in the sky as they hunt insects.

Long, forked tail has thin, streamer-like feathers

Pheasant

When startled, it rockets into the air, calling 'kok, kok, kok'. Female birds are speckled brown.

This is a male pheasant

Yellowhammer

Likes open country. The rhythm of its song sounds like 'a little bit of bread and no cheeeese'.

Forms flocks in winter

Nests on the ground in open areas

Skylark

Watch for male skylarks flying straight up to a great height, then hovering to sing with a clear warble.

Cuckoo

Found all over Europe in summer. Listen for the male's falling 'cuckoo' call.

Female has a bubbling call

Owls and night birds

You can't see its long ear tufts while it flies

Long-eared owl

A shy bird that hides among branches in thick pine woods. It hunts at night and sleeps in the day.

Flies in zig-zags as it hunts

Sometimes perches on the ground

Short-eared owl

You might spot this fierce-looking owl in daylight or at dusk, hunting over open fields and moorland.

Barn owl

Flies low over fields at night, hunting small animals that rustle in the grass. Its call is a shrill shriek.

Nests in old buildings or hollow trees

Little owl

This small, flat-headed owl bobs up and down when curious. It flies low over farmland and hunts at dusk.

Nests in tree-holes

Tawny owl

Listen for them hooting after dark. Male owls call, 'whoo, tu-whoo' and the females answer, 'tu-whit'.

Often hunts near woodlands

Nightjar

This bird nests on heathland in summer, hunting insects at night. It has a churring two-note call.

Spends the winter in Africa

Water birds

Mallard

Male ducks make a soft 'crrb crrb' sound. Speckled brown females call 'quack quack'.

Lives on rivers, canals, ponds and lakes

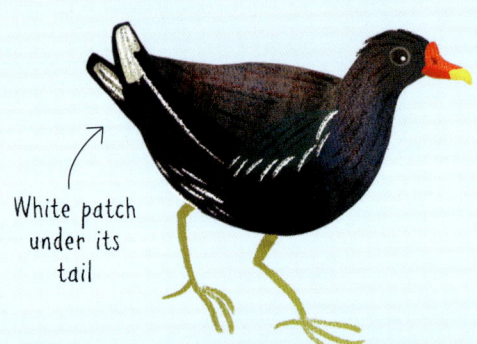

White patch under its tail

Moorhen

Look for its red beak with a yellow tip. It makes 'kreck-kreck-kreck' and 'kyorrl' calls.

Mute swan

A very large bird that lives by lakes or rivers. It hisses and flaps aggressively to protect its territory.

Young swans are brown

Kingfisher

Very small, with bright, shimmering feathers. It dives for fish in streams and rivers.

Listen for its shrill whistle

Canada goose

Look in parks for this large goose with a noisy, honking call.

Often seen in big groups

Grey heron

You might see one standing very still near a river or lake, waiting to spear fish with its sharp beak.

Its huge wings flap slowly in flight

Wading birds

Oystercatcher

Usually seen near the sea, especially in winter. It feeds on shellfish. Listen for its loud 'peep' call.

Opens shells with its beak

Golden plover

This golden-feathered bird breeds on upland moors. It's found in flocks on coastal marshes or lowland farms in winter.

Curlew

Nests on moors and upland farms. You might spot it on the coast at other times of year. Its call sounds like 'courli'.

White patch underneath

Common sandpiper

Look for them near upland streams and lakes in summer, and wet, lowland areas in spring and autumn.

Its tail bobs up and down

Lapwing

Forms flocks on farmland in winter. In spring, look out for males twisting and tumbling in the air, calling 'peee-wit'.

Looks black and white from a distance

Dunlin

Dunlins often visit the seashore, but they nest on moorland in the north. Frequently seen in flocks.

Feathers are grey in winter

Birds of prey

Peregrine falcon

Builds its nest on sea cliffs, inland crags, or sometimes even tall city buildings. It dives on flying birds at record-breaking speed.

Buzzard

This large, broad-winged bird soars over moors and farmland as it hunts. Listen for its 'mew' call.

Watch for it gliding in wide, slow circles

Kestrel

Look up above fields and roadside verges to see them hovering in one place, then swooping down to catch prey.

Red kite

Soars for long periods of time, landing to feed when it spots dead animals or other prey on the ground below.

Look for deeply forked tail

Female is larger, with browner feathers

Sparrowhawk

An agile hunter. It never hovers, but darts between trees in woods and sometimes even in gardens, catching small birds.

Golden eagle

Huge, majestic golden eagles live in the Scottish Highlands, gliding far over forests and mountainsides.

Builds huge nests in trees or on rocky cliffs

Wingspan can be wider than a car

Town trees

Leyland cypress

Often used for hedges because it grows very quickly and doesn't drop its leaves in winter.

Tiny, scaly leaves

Flowers in spring

Horse chestnut

Wander under this tree in autumn and hunt for conkers on the ground. You'll find them nestled inside spiky green cases.

Conker in its case

London plane

A common sight in London – and other big cities too. Walk the streets in autumn and see its amber leaves on the wet pavement.

'Bobble fruits' stay on tree through winter

Winged seeds

Norway maple

This handsome tree has seeds with leafy wings. Watch them slowly fall, twirling on a gust of autumn wind.

Common lime

Grows soft, heart-shaped leaves and little green fruits on long stalks.

Blossom in early summer

Eucalyptus

Its silvery-green leaves stay on through winter, and grow longer, greener and more pointy as the years go by.

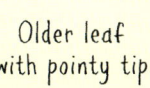

Older leaf with pointy tip

Park trees

Sycamore

A big, spreading tree with leathery leaves. Watch its winged seeds spinning to the ground on blustery autumn days.

Leaves have toothed edges

Common walnut

You'll see squirrels collecting the green cases that drop from its branches in autumn. They're after the wrinkly walnuts inside.

Each leaf has 7-9 leaflets

Cedar of Lebanon

Often seen in parks and stately gardens. Its flat branches spread like great green stepping stones into the sky.

Cone

Lawson cypress

Can be shaped into a thick, evergreen hedge. Its leaves look like scaly insect legs, and smell like sour parsley.

Pea-sized cones grow on twig tips

Whitebeam

Seems to flicker as the wind lifts the pale underside of its leaves. The birds love its red berries in autumn.

Bright red berries

Monkey puzzle or Chile pine

These trees were around in prehistoric times. Their sharp leaves stopped grazing dinosaurs from stripping their branches bare.

Thick, sharp evergreen leaves

Hedgerow trees

Common pear

Grows in gardens and also in the wild. Look for its sweet, golden fruits on autumn walks in the country.

Pears often have a gritty texture

Crab apple

Has gnarled, lichen-covered branches. Its blossom smells sweet and rosy, and its fruit makes tangy jellies and jams.

Leaves have a toothed edge

Hazel

Smallish tree with smooth, bendy branches and soft leaves. Squirrels and dormice love its tasty nuts.

Nuts have a hard brown shell

Berries poisonous for people

Holly

Glossy, evergreen leaves – watch out for the prickles! Its red berries are easy to spot in the dark winter months.

Elder

Its clusters of tiny white flowers smell like springtime. The berries shouldn't be eaten raw, but are used in wine and jam.

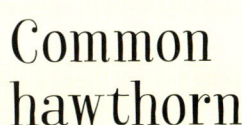

Common hawthorn

One of the first trees to waken after winter. Its pale, delicate flowers herald the coming of spring.

Red berries, called haws, on thorny branches

Woodland trees

Common beech

Wander through a beech wood in autumn and feel the empty nut husks crunching underfoot. The trunks rise like grey columns beneath copper-coloured leaves.

Nut has a hairy 'husk'

Common ash

Look for its black, velvety leaf buds in winter, and bunches of winged fruits, called keys, in autumn.

Keys fall in winter and early spring

English oak

This mighty tree grows in the heart of the forest. Look up into its wide, crooked branches and see all the woodland creatures that call it home.

Acorns grow in little 'cups'

Sweet chestnut

Hunt for its soft, sweet nuts to roast in winter. Their prickly green cases lie half-hidden in the fallen leaves.

Yellow flowers that smell of mushrooms

Tangy fruits, called chequers

Wild service tree

Explore the hidden dells of ancient woodland and find this rare tree growing alongside gnarled old oaks and graceful ash.

Yew

Lives longer than any other tree in Britain – some are over 1,000 years old. Find them in quiet churchyards, watching over the graves.

Leaves and 'berries' very poisonous

31

Woodland trees

Papery, green-winged fruits

Hornbeam

Look for its gnarled branches and twisted trunk. It's often covered in copper-coloured leaves all through winter, and has the hardest wood of any tree in Britain.

Larch

The only conifer tree in Britain that drops its needles. In autumn, larch forests set mountainsides ablaze as they turn from green to gold.

Cones stay on all winter

Cones dangle down →

Douglas fir

Thrives in wild, rainy places. Its forests are dark and mossy, with great, towering trees many centuries old.

Silver birch

A delicate tree with white, papery bark and drooping branches. In spring, its small leaves flutter above sun-dappled woodland flowers.

Long flowers, called catkins

Wild cherry

In early spring the branches shine with white blossom. Then over summer its red fruits darken until they're almost black and ready to eat.

Cherries have long stems

Small-leaved lime

A shapely tree often planted in stately gardens. It's become rare in the wild, but still grows in ancient woodland. Bees love its sweet-smelling nectar.

Heart-shaped leaves

Trees near water

Tops of leaves are darker green

White poplar

Thrives on windswept coasts. Its pale leaves are almost white underneath, and flicker brightly on warm summer days.

Bird cherry

Likes damp woodland and riverbanks. Its nectar smells like marzipan, and birds love its bitter black fruit.

Flowers and cherries grow on short stalks

Narrow, pointed leaves

Weeping willow

Easily recognized by its long, yellow twigs that droop down to the ground and sway softly in the breeze.

Crack willow

A scruffy-looking tree with brittle branches. Listen for the loud 'crack' when they break.

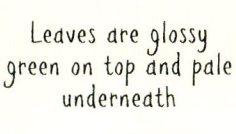

Leaves are glossy green on top and pale underneath →

Long, bendy stems ↘

Aspen

A slender, sun-loving tree that shimmers in the slightest breeze. Listen for the rustle of its rippling leaves.

Rivers help spread its seeds

Common alder

Likes the sort of wet, marshy ground that would rot most trees. Look for it beside rivers and lakes, and see its long roots reaching down into the water.

Moorland trees

Juniper

A small, bushy evergreen tree with prickly needles. Its blue-black berries give jams and cordials a sharp, woody flavour with a hint of spice.

Berries can take three years to ripen

Scots pine

Towers over the windswept heath like a mighty sentinel. Its bare trunk has greyish, flaky bark that turns rusty-brown higher up the tree.

Closed cones are pointed

Field maple

Likes low, rolling hills and parkland. Its winged seeds twirl in the autumn wind, and in late winter its sap makes sweet, amber syrup.

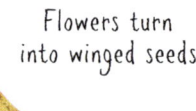

Flowers turn into winged seeds

Purging buckthorn

A small, prickly tree with glossy leaves. Its dark berries are liked by birds, but give people an upset stomach.

Dark, toothed leaves

Blackthorn

As winter ends, watch for white flowers blooming on its bare, thorny branches. The leaves appear later in the spring.

Inky-blue berries, called sloes

Clusters of pale flowers in spring

Spindle

Grows in hedges and the edges of ancient woodland. Easy to spot in autumn and winter with its delicate pink fruits with orange seeds.

Wetland trees

Swamp cypress

Prefers swampy ground beside lakes and rivers. Look for its knobbly 'knees' poking up from underwater roots like snorkels to help it breathe.

Its soft needles drop in autumn

Downy birch

Delicate-looking, but as tough as they come. It grows in wet, high places – and further north than any other broadleaf tree.

Leaf stalks and twigs are furry to the touch

Black poplar

This tree is now very rare, and grows alone on damp, boggy ground. Look for its fluffy seeds in late summer – they look like big tufts of cotton wool.

Shiny, heart-shaped leaves

Bay willow

A dainty willow with dark, glossy leaves that lives by streams and rivers. Watch its fluffy seeds float away on the water in late summer.

Green catkins turn white and fluffy

Alder buckthorn

A small tree that makes a big bang – its bark is used in gunpowder. It thrives in open woods and wet heathland.

Berries ripen to dark purple or black

Long, thin leaves

Osier willow

Find it by rivers and streams. Feel the silvery fuzz on the back of its leaves, and see how far you can bend one of its long, yellow twigs. They're often woven into baskets.

Upland trees

Creamy-white flowers in spring

Rowan

In winter, see a lone rowan on the snow-covered hills. Its bunches of red berries feed the moorland birds.

Copper beech

Easy to spot in spring and summer with its deep purple leaves, which turn coppery-brown in autumn.

Woody case with edible nut inside

Sessile oak

Find this majestic tree on strolls through wooded hills. Its name means 'stalkless oak' because its acorns have no stalks.

Acorns green in spring, brown in autumn

Western hemlock

Grown in square, dark forests on hills, where it's planted like a crop for its wood. The forests are very quiet, because not much can grow in the heavy shade beneath the branches.

Long, drooping branches

Wych elm

Sadly a rare sight these days, as many have been killed by Dutch elm disease, but can still be found, especially in hilly or rocky woodlands to the north.

Leaves have long points

Sitka spruce

Grows in large plantations on rainswept northern hillsides, where its dense branches provide shelter for weasels and foxes.

Needles are very prickly

41

Coastal trees

Tamarisk

Small and tough, it thrives on dry, salty ground. Take a walk along the coast in late summer and see the tiny pink flowers that cling to its wiry branches.

Grows well in windy places

Holm oak

Look for this smallish oak on warm southern coasts. It doesn't mind the salt spray, so can shield houses and gardens from the harsh sea wind.

Small pointy acorns

Sea buckthorn

One of the toughest plants around. Clings to sand dunes through frozen winters and dry summers, then blazes with bright orange berries every autumn.

Clusters of small, bitter berries

Monterey pine

Grows well in dry, sandy soil, because its roots can burrow very deep underground to find water.

Cones only open in forest fires, so new trees can grow from the seeds

Monterey cypress

Likes cool, wet conditions by the coast. See it looming through the sea mist on chilly winter mornings. Its scaly leaves smell like lemons when crushed.

Often planted in parks and gardens

Austrian pine

Towers over dunes and open heathland, its long needles rustling in the wind. Shelter in its deep shade on hot summer days.

Narrow cones open when ripe

Garden bugs

7-spot ladybird

Look in gardens, hedges, woods and meadows. It hibernates during colder months in cracks in sheds, houses or tree bark. March–October.

Buff-tailed bumblebee

Watch for them buzzing between flowers in summer, feeding on nectar. They also collect pollen, in tiny yellow leg-pouches. February–October.

Nests in holes in the ground

Small tortoise-shell butterfly

These butterflies wake from hibernation in spring, then females lay big heaps of eggs on the underside of nettle leaves. March–November.

Blue spots along wing edges

Green lacewing

You'll spot these in gardens and hedges, and sometimes indoors, attracted by house lights. They hibernate in sheds or houses. April–October.

Gets its name from its delicate, see-through wings

Caterpillar is known as a 'woolly bear'

Garden tiger moth

Mostly active at night. Its caterpillars are fuzzy and may make your skin itch, so don't touch them. June–September.

Devil's coach horse beetle

Comes out at night, resting in leaf litter or under stones in the day. It lifts its tail and spreads its jaws if threatened. April–October.

Very speedy runner

Garden bugs

Peacock butterfly

The 'eye' markings on its wings help to scare enemies. It looks like a dead leaf when its wings are shut.

Drinks nectar from buddleia and other flowers

Look for its large pincers

Common earwig

Earwigs sleep in damp places such as under stones during the day, coming out at night to feed.

Black ant

You'll see ants scuttling around collecting food. Males and queens have wings, and fly out of the nest in mid-summer to mate. June–August.

Likes fruit and other sweet things

Bee fly

Try and spot this fly's long, tube-like mouthparts, which it uses to drink nectar from flowers. April–June.

Doesn't bite or sting

Red admiral butterfly

These bright butterflies are often seen collecting nectar from flowering ivy and Michaelmas daisies. May–October.

White spots along wing edges

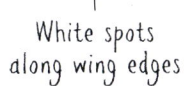

Hoverfly

Its markings make it look a bit like a wasp, but don't worry – it doesn't sting. Look out for it hovering in the air. March–November.

Listen for the hum of its wings

Park bugs

Common wasp

Watch for them buzzing around your summer picnics – they feed on sweet things, as well as other insects. April–October.

Most likely to sting in late summer

Small white butterfly

This butterfly is often known as a 'cabbage white', because that's what its caterpillars eat. May–August.

Black spots may be fainter in late summer

Vapourer moth

Males have rusty brown wings with two white spots. Females only have wing stubs and can't fly. July–September.

Flies during the day

Cinnabar moth

Look on waste ground and railway banks for this moth, which sometimes flies in the day as well as at night. May–August.

Often rests in long grass

Cockchafer or Maybug

A large beetle that flies around treetops. You might also see them flying down chimneys or against lighted windows. April–June.

Spot its feathery feelers

22-spot ladybird

This tiny ladybird eats mould that grows on soil and low-growing plants. April–August.

Look under leaves close to the ground

Woodland bugs

Stag beetle

You're most likely to see one in southern England. Male stag beetles have huge jaws that look like antlers. May–September.

Horse fly

The female horse fly sucks blood, but her loud hum usually warns you before you are bitten. May–September.

Most active in bright, sunny places

Hornet

This striped stinging insect is much larger than a wasp. It nests in hollow trees, banks or roofs. May–November.

Females chew up wood to make nests

Green shield bug

Spot these bugs on leaves, basking in the sun, especially on trees such as hazel and birch. May–October.

Turns green-bronze later in the year

Violet ground beetle

This fierce, fast-running predator rests during the day in leaf litter or under logs or stones, coming out to hunt at night. March–October.

Eats other insects, slugs and worms

Horned treehopper

A thorny-looking bug that jumps along twigs and low plants in woods. It feeds on oak leaves and other plants. April–August.

Woodland bugs

Poplar hawk moth

A very big, night-flying moth. Its front wings stick out over its back wings while it rests. May–August.

Blends in with leaves when it's resting

Peach blossom moth

This moth's name comes from the pattern on its wings. It flies at night, and is attracted to light and sugar. June–September.

Spends winter hibernating in sheds or barns

Herald moth

Flies at night and rests among dead leaves by day. Look for the bright orange patches on its wings. March–November.

Purple emperor butterfly

The large purple males fly around treetops, sometimes fluttering down to drink from woodland puddles. July–August.

Females are brown

Wasp beetle

This striped beetle looks a bit like a wasp, but it's harmless. It flies in bright sunshine, visiting flowers. May–August.

Wasp-like appearance puts off hunters

Has knobbly black feelers

Red-headed cardinal beetle

Look for it sunbathing on flowers, tree trunks and stumps, where it also hunts other insects. May–July.

Grassland bugs

Field grasshopper

Males 'chirrup' as they rub their legs against their wings. Look in short vegetation on sunny days. May–October.

Eats plants and grasses

Glow worm

Wingless female glow worms sit on blades of grass at dusk and attract males with their glowing tails. May–August.

Male

Feeds on slugs and snails

Female

Watch for them hovering in the air

Ghost moth

You might spot males flying at dusk, searching for the yellow-winged females in dense grass. June–July.

Common blue butterfly

Watch for them flying on sunny days. They rest head-down on blades of grass when it's wet or cloudy. June–September.

Females are mostly brown

Green tortoise beetle

Pulls its legs and antennae in when threatened, so it looks like a tiny tortoise. Its diet includes white dead-nettles. April–October.

Feet grip leaves very tightly

Dor beetle

With a loud droning sound, this big beetle flies to dung heaps at night, where it will eat its own weight in dung. April–October.

Domed, shiny black body

Meadow bugs

Black and red froghopper

Search in dense grass and on trees. It holds its wing cases up to form a tent shape over its body while it rests. April–June.

Hunts smaller insects

Common malachite beetle

Look in buttercups and other flowers. Smelly orange pouches bulge from its sides when alarmed, to put off enemies. April–August.

Green leafhopper

Males are turquoise or black, and females are green. They feed on grasses and rushes, and communicate with faint clicks. May–September.

Meadow brown butterfly

Visits thistles and bramble flowers, even on dull days. Females have large orange patches on each of their four wings. June–September.

Wing spots have one white dot inside

Marbled white butterfly

Watch for it visiting purple flowers such as thistles, knapweed and field scabious. June–August.

Likes areas with long grass

Oil beetle

This large beetle can't fly, so it's often trodden on as it walks along paths and clifftops. It oozes drops of oily liquid when alarmed. March–May.

Pond bugs

Backswimmer

Search in pools, canals and ditches. It jerks along with its hind legs, usually on its back, catching tadpoles and small fish to eat.

Back legs work like paddles

Pond skater

This spindly bug 'skates' across the water's surface, picking up dead or dying insects with its short front legs. April–October.

Long legs hold it up above the water

Water measurer

Lives at the edges of ponds, slow rivers and streams. It hunts smaller insects, stabbing them with its sharp mouthparts.

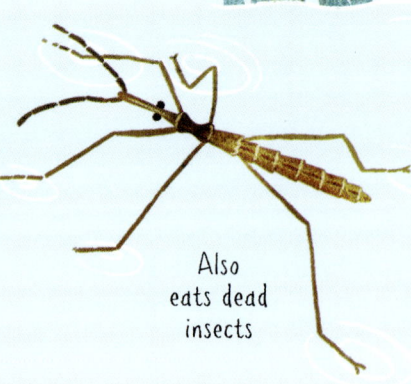

Also eats dead insects

Whirligig beetle

These beetles gather in groups on the surface of still or slow-moving water in bright sunshine, swimming in frantic circles. July–September.

Dives underwater if disturbed

Common blue damselfly

Look in vegetation near water. A female's body is duller blue or green, with black stripes. April–September.

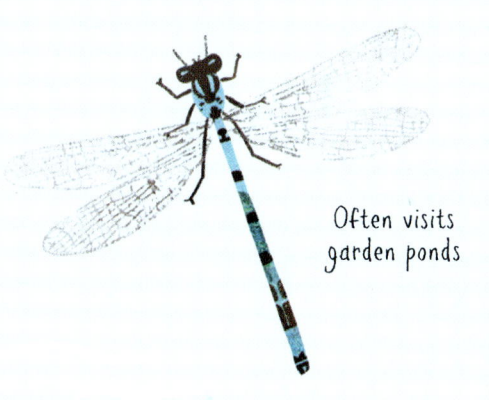

Often visits garden ponds

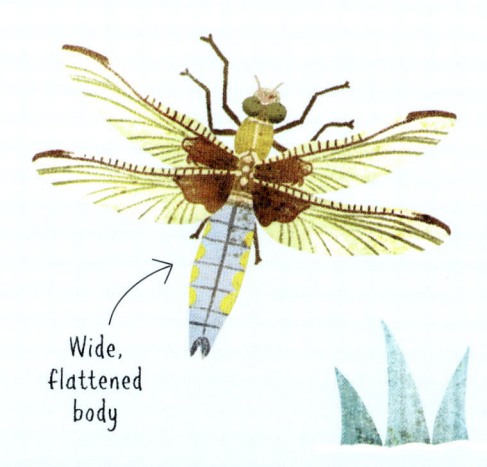

Broad-bodied chaser

You might spot one over a pond or lake with plenty of plants. They fly in short bursts as they hunt insects, often returning to the same perch. May–August.

Wide, flattened body

Wetland bugs

Mayfly

Adult lives are short, often only a few hours. In this time they mate, and females lay their eggs on the water's surface.

Spot its three long tails

Banded demoiselle

Look near canals, streams and rivers with muddy bottoms. Males perch on plants and flutter their wings to attract a mate. May–August.

Shiny, metallic body

Golden-ringed dragonfly

A fast and powerful flier. It lives near streams and rivers, but is sometimes seen far from water. May–September.

The UK's longest dragonfly

Emperor dragonfly

Spot these big dragonflies gliding and swooping over large ponds, lakes and canals, catching flies in mid-air. June–October.

Females are dull green

Attracted to lights at night

Giant crane fly

Often found near water, these weak fliers wobble about in the air. They're sometimes called 'Daddy-long-legs'. April–August.

Brimstone butterfly

Its leaf-shaped wings give camouflage when resting on plants and hedges. Females are pale greeny-white.

Look for small orange wing spots

Moorland bugs

Heath assassin bug

A fierce hunter that catches other insects, then sucks out their body fluids. Look on open heaths and sand dunes. June–October.

Green tiger beetle

This bright green beetle runs quickly along the ground, and flies, buzzing, for short distances if disturbed. April–September.

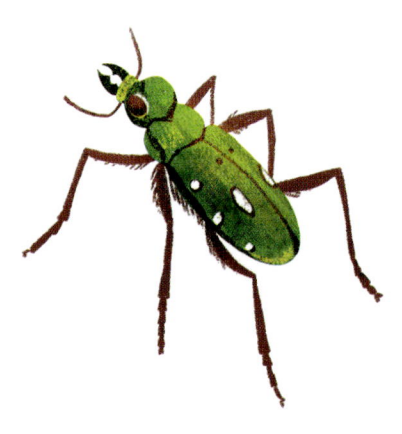

Minotaur beetle

You're most likely to spot these in sandy places, especially where rabbits live – they eat rabbit dung. Males have three bull-like horns. September–July.

Ridged wing-cases are glossy black

Male has feathery feelers

Emperor moth

Easy to recognize thanks to the 'eye' markings on their wings. Males flutter around during the day, while females rest on low plants. March–May.

Silver-studded blue butterfly

Look out for them flying near heather. Males are blue, and females are brown. June–August.

Also lives on clifftop grassland and sand dunes

Large heath butterfly

Visits heath flowers, resting on grasses with wings closed if the weather is too warm, sunny or windy. June–August.

Likes damp, boggy areas

63

Creepy crawlies

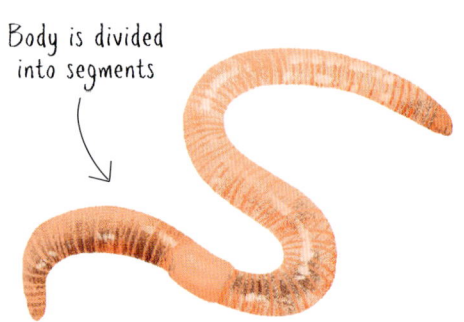

Body is divided into segments

Earthworm

You might spot them on the soil's surface after rain, but they're usually underground, tunnelling through the earth.

Common centipede

Its name means '100 feet', but this kind of centipede only has fifteen pairs of legs. Find it under stones or plant pots.

Hunts insects, slugs and spiders

Shell protects its soft body

Garden snail

If you find holes in your plants, they might have been nibbled by one of these. They come out at night, when it's cool and damp.

Garden spider

Their webs are easiest to spot on misty mornings, when tiny water droplets gather on the silky strands. April–November.

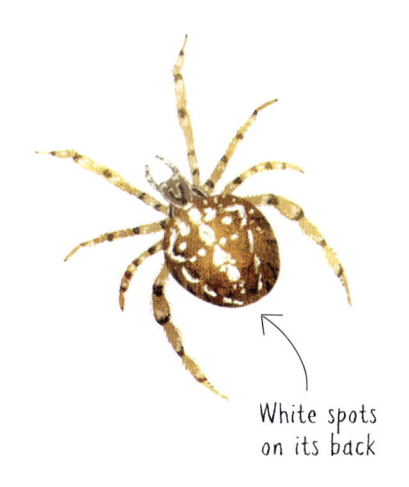

White spots on its back

Lift up logs or stones to find them

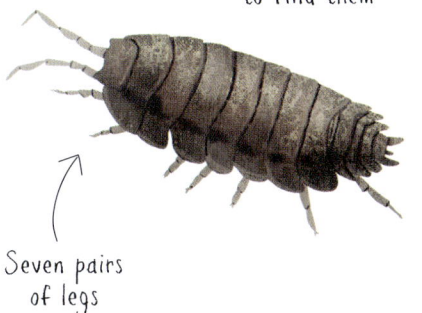

Common woodlouse

These helpful creepy-crawlies tidy up the garden by eating rotten wood, dead leaves and other decaying things.

Seven pairs of legs

Garden slug

There can be thousands of slugs in a single garden! They spend the daytime under the soil and in other dark, damp places.

Look for their silvery trails in the morning

Town flowers

Daisy

Search for this little plant amongst the grass on a lawn. Its flowers close at night and in rain to keep the pollen dry. January–October.

Rosebay willowherb

A tall plant with spikes of pink flowers and long, narrow leaves. It's common on railway banks and disused land. July–September.

Lots may grow together

Dandelion clock

Dandelion

This common weed will grow almost anywhere. Look for its toothed leaves and downy white 'clock' of seeds. March–June.

Houseleek

A rosette plant with fleshy leaves and dull-red, spiky petals. Look on old walls and roofs. It does not flower every year. June–July.

Usually you will only see the houseleek's rosette without a stalk

Ivy-leaved toadflax

Slender stalks trail on old walls. Look for the yellow parts on its mauve flowers. May–September.

Stems can have a reddish tinge

Stinging nettle

Easy to find in all kinds of places. It has toothed leaves covered with stinging hairs, and dangling green-brown flowers. June–August.

Hedgerow flowers

Dog rose

A creeping plant with thorny stems and sweet-smelling flowers. Look for its red fruits, called rosehips, in autumn. June–July.

Fruit

Cow parsley

You'll see this tall plant around hedgebanks and ditches. It has ribbed stems, feathery leaves and white flower clusters. May–June.

Small pink flowers have five petals

Herb Robert

A spreading, low-growing plant with a strong smell. Its stems and leaves turn red as the year goes on. May–September.

A ripe berry is purplish-black

Blackberry

This dense, woody plant climbs up hedges. It has sharp prickles, and edible berries that ripen in autumn. June–September.

White dead-nettle

This nettle's hairy leaves do not sting. Spot its white or greenish-white flowers. March–November.

Flowers grow up the main stem

Honeysuckle

Look for this climbing plant twining through trees and shrubs. Its sweet-smelling, creamy flowers are tinged with orange, red or lilac. May–August.

Meadow flowers

Creeping buttercup

Grows in spreading clumps. Look close to the ground for its long, trailing stems and shiny yellow flowers. May–August.

Meadow thistle

A small thistle with dark red or purple flowers and prickly leaves. It prefers damp, boggy areas. June–August.

Leaves and stem are hairy

Cowslip

Easily recognized by the single clusters of drooping flowers. Look in sunny, grassy places. April–May.

Dark green, wrinkly leaves

Oxeye daisy

You'll often see masses of these big white and yellow flowers on tall, upright stems covering roadside verges. June–September.

Grows best in sunny spots

Fritillary or Snake's head

Spot these drooping, bell-shaped, chequered flowers blooming in woods and damp meadows in May.

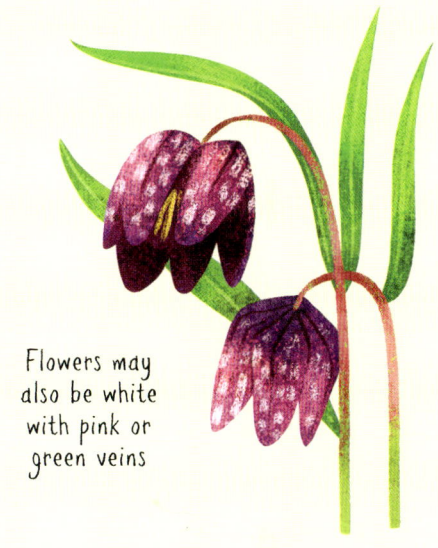

Flowers may also be white with pink or green veins

Red clover

Bees love to drink nectar from pompom-shaped clover flowers, which can be light or dark pink. May–October.

Oval leaves have pale patches

Woodland flowers

Primrose

A spring flower with a hairy stem and wrinkled leaves. It grows in patches in woods, hedges and fields. December–May.

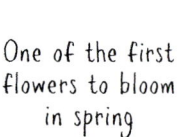

One of the first flowers to bloom in spring

Foxglove

An upright plant with a tall spike of trumpet-shaped flowers, drooping on one side of the stem. June–September.

Very poisonous – don't touch

Wood anemone

You might see carpets of these flowers growing in woods. Look for pink streaks on the outside of the petals. March–June.

Red campion

This upright woodland plant has a hairy, sticky stem and opposite pairs of pointed, oval leaves. May–June.

Buds are dark red

Wood woundwort

Look for spikes of dark red flowers in woods, hedgerows and roadsides. Its toothed leaves give off a strong, unpleasant smell. June–August.

Flowers and leaves are hairy

Spur points backwards

Common dog violet

A creeping woodland plant with heart-shaped leaves and short spurs on its purple flowers. April–June.

Woodland flowers

Lesser celandine

A small, creeping plant with shiny yellow flowers. Look in damp, shady woods and on roadsides. March–May.

Glossy, heart-shaped leaves

Yellow archangel

Look for the red-brown markings on the yellow petals. Its toothed leaves grow opposite each other in pairs. May–June.

Snowdrop

You might see these nodding, honey-scented white flowers blooming even on snowy days. January–March.

Yellow pimpernel

Its star-shaped yellow flowers and oval or heart-shaped leaves grow on slender, trailing stems. May–September.

Look in damp woods

Bluebell

Spot the narrow, shiny leaves and clusters of nodding, bell-shaped flowers. They form thick carpets in woods. April–May.

Flowers hang on arched stems

Bugle

A creeping plant with upright flower spikes and hairy, purplish stems. It forms carpets in damp woods. May–June.

Purple patches on leaves

Pond and river flowers

Flat leaves are known as lily pads

White water-lily

Look for blankets of floating leaves on still or slow-moving water. Its white flowers are deeply cup-shaped. June–September.

Yellow water-lily

Forms leafy mats on slow-moving water. Yellow, cup-shaped flowers are held out of the water on long, firm stems. June–September.

Flowers can be pink, purple or white

Policeman's helmet

Spot its flowers that look like open mouths. Its ripe seed pods burst when touched. July–October.

Thin, crumpled petals

Frogbit

This plant rises to the surface of ponds and canals in spring. Its shiny round leaves grow in tufts. July–August.

Purple loosestrife

A tall plant with a hairy stem and leaves. It grows in clumps by rivers and streams, and on marshes. June–September.

Flowers have five or six petals

Water crowfoot

Anchors its roots in mud at the bottom of ponds and streams, while flowers cover the water's surface. May–June.

Feathery leaves float under the water

Seashore flowers

Golden samphire
Grows on sea cliffs and salt marshes. Look for the large yellow flower heads and narrow, fleshy leaves. July–August.

Arching 'horns' are seedpods

Yellow horned poppy
You might see these growing on shingle beaches. They have flimsy yellow flowers, and toothed leaves. June–October.

Bloody cranesbill
This bushy plant has deeply divided leaves on hairy stems, and bright, pinkish-purple flowers. June–August.

Viper's bugloss

Look for its blue flowers that open from pink buds. It likes sand dunes and other dry, open, stony places. June–September.

Rough leaves grow on bristly stems

Thrift

This plant grows in dense mats of grass-like leaves with small, pink flowers. May–August.

Look on coastal rocks and salt marshes

Sea aster

You'll find this fleshy plant growing on salt marshes and sea cliffs. Its flowers look like mauve or lilac daisies, and grow in loose clusters. July–October.

Spear-shaped leaves

Moorland flowers

Heath speedwell

Grows close to the ground in grassy places and woods. Its flowers grow in upright spikes. May–August.

Oval leaves are hairy

Goldenrod

An upright plant with stiff, leafy stems and flowers on thin spikes. Look in woods and on heaths and rocky ground. July–September.

Gorse

You'll find this dark green, spiny bush on heaths and commons. Its bright yellow flowers smell of coconut and vanilla. March–June.

Spiky leaves stay green all year

Heather or Ling

Carpets large areas of heaths and moors. Its leafy spikes of tiny pink or white flowers are shaped like bells. July–September.

Stems are woody and tough

Harebell

This plant has slender, branching stems with bell-shaped flowers. Look on heaths and grassland. June–September.

Violet-blue flowers hang down

A creeping plant

Bird's-foot trefoil

Gets its name from its seed pods, which look like a bird's claws. Spot the thin red streaks on its yellow flowers. May–September.

Marsh flowers

Meadowsweet

Its frothy clusters of flowers smell sweet. Look in marshes, damp grassland, and by streams and ditches. May–September.

Marsh violet

This plant has lilac flowers with dark purple veins, and heart- or kidney-shaped leaves. April–July.

Grows low to the ground

Marsh marigold

Look for clumps of it growing in wet places. It has shiny yellow flowers and large, heart-shaped leaves. March–June.

Great willowherb

Forms large patches in riverbanks and ditches. Its tall stems have pink, or sometimes white, flowers. June–September.

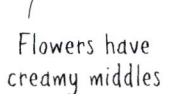

Flowers have creamy middles

Devil's-bit scabious

Found in wet, grassy places, this plant's bluish-purple, domed flower heads grow on long stalks. June–October.

Ragged Robin

Pink flowers with ragged petals grow on upright, forked stems. Look in marshes and damp places. May–June.

Narrow, pointed leaves

Flowers on bare ground

Larkspur

This slender plant has spikes of purple, pink or white flowers. A long spur sticks out behind each flower. June–July.

Feathery leaves

Flower heads are made up of many tiny flowers

Cornflower

Look for them in farm fields. The blue flower heads appear above scaly, cup-shaped parts. July–August.

St. John's wort

Has clusters of deep yellow flowers. The see-through dots on its petals look like tiny holes. June–September.

Narrow, oval leaves

Wild pansy

Its bright flowers grow low to the ground, and can be any mixture of purple, yellow and white. April–October.

Wavy-edged, oval leaves

Common poppy

You might see whole fields of these soft red flowers blooming on farmland in summer. June–August.

Round seed pods grow in late summer

Greater bindweed

Climbs walls and hedges, its stems twining around anything they meet. Its funnel-shaped flowers are pink or white. July–September.

Mammals

Red fox

You might see a red fox in the early morning or late evening. Its bushy tail is known as a brush.

Often found in towns and cities

Rabbit

Watch for its fluffy white tail bobbing as it runs. It likes to nibble on grasses, young plants and tree bark.

Rabbits live in big groups, in burrows called warrens

Buries nuts to eat in winter

Grey squirrel

Easy to spot scampering around woodlands, parks and gardens. Look out for its bushy grey tail.

Pipistrelle bat

Darts and twists through the air, snapping up flying insects – up to 3,000 in a single night. April–October.

Very small and light

Hedgehog

This spiky little animal snuffles about in gardens and parks after dark, hunting for slugs. March–November.

Rolls into a prickly ball when frightened

House mouse

House mice can be found living wherever humans do, in holes and tunnels, especially in older buildings.

Large ears

Mostly active at night

Mammals

Badger

Badgers live underground in large burrows called setts, which they dig with their powerful paws.

Only comes out at night

Weasel

Watch for this small, slender animal darting along the ground under the cover of plants and bushes.

Long body and short legs

Fallow deer

These deer graze on acorns, grass, bark and berries. They're easily startled, so if you see one, stay still and quiet.

Males' antlers fall off and regrow each year

Common shrew

A tiny creature with a long, pointed nose. It snuffles through fallen leaves, hunting bugs and worms.

Very small ears and eyes

Has tufts of fur on its ears

Red squirrel

This rare, shy squirrel is smaller than a grey squirrel. It loves to nibble the seeds from pine cones.

Brown rat

Mostly lives underground, but you might spot one darting along looking for food – it will eat almost anything.

Tail is long and scaly

Amphibians and reptiles

Lays eggs in ponds in spring

Common frog
Its smooth green or brown skin can become lighter or darker for camouflage. February–October.

Grass snake
Often seen swimming in ponds, or sunbathing nearby. It does not bite or harm humans. April–October.

Greenish skin with dark markings

Smooth newt
Look for it in cool, damp places, such as under logs. March–October.

Great crested newt

This large newt has rough, knobbly skin, with black spots on its orange belly. March–October.

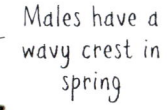

Males have a wavy crest in spring

Common toad

Wide and stocky, with copper-coloured eyes. Hunts slugs and snails at night. February–October.

Warty, green-brown skin

Palmate newt

In spring, you might spot it visiting ponds on heaths or moors to lay its eggs. March–October.

Underside is yellowy-orange

Freshwater fish

Look for its red fins and tail

Perch
You might spot some of these fish swimming together in a group (or shoal). They like clean, shaded water.

Three-spined stickleback
A small but aggressive hunter, with three sharp spines on its back, and silvery scales on its sides and belly.

Male's belly turns red in spring

Tench
Usually hides among weeds at the bottom of lakes and slow-flowing rivers, or lies buried in the mud.

Has thick, slimy, slippery skin

Minnow

Watch for large shoals of these tiny fish in clear, flowing water such as streams and rivers.

A fast, darting fish

Carp

Likes to bask in the sun near the surface of weed-filled lakes. Look for the whisker-like barbels (feelers) near its mouth.

Heavy, rounded body

Pike

This fast, fierce hunter lurks in dense weed. It uses its huge jaws to catch fish, frogs, small mammals and even water birds.

Can be over a metre long

Index

7-spot ladybird, 44
22-spot ladybird, 49

Alder buckthorn, 39
Aspen, 35
Austrian pine, 43

Backswimmer, 58
Badger, 88
Banded demoiselle, 60
Barn owl, 16
Bay willow, 39
Bee fly, 47
Bird cherry, 34
Bird's-foot trefoil, 81
Black and red froghopper, 56
Black ant, 46
Blackberry, 69
Blackbird, 7
Blackcap, 10
Black poplar, 38
Blackthorn, 37
Bloody cranesbill, 78
Bluebell, 75
Blue tit, 5
Brimstone butterfly, 61
Broad-bodied chaser, 59
Brown rat, 89
Buff-tailed bumblebee, 44
Bugle, 75
Bullfinch, 4
Buzzard, 22

Canada goose, 19
Carp, 93
Carrion crow, 13
Cedar of Lebanon, 26
Chaffinch, 4
Cinnabar moth, 49
Coal tit, 12
Cockchafer, 49
Collared dove, 7
Common alder, 35
Common ash, 30
Common beech, 30
Common blue butterfly, 55
Common blue damselfly, 59
Common centipede, 64
Common dog violet, 73
Common earwig, 46
Common frog, 90
Common hawthorn, 29
Common lime, 25
Common malachite beetle, 56
Common pear, 28
Common poppy, 85
Common sandpiper, 21
Common shrew, 89
Common toad, 91
Common walnut, 26
Common wasp, 48
Common woodlouse, 65
Copper beech, 40
Cornflower, 84
Cow parsley, 68

Cowslip, 70
Crab apple, 28
Crack willow, 35
Creeping buttercup, 70
Cuckoo, 15
Curlew, 20

Daisy, 66
Dandelion, 66
Devil's-bit scabious, 83
Devil's coach horse beetle, 45
Dog rose, 68
Dor beetle, 55
Douglas fir, 32
Downy birch, 38
Dunlin, 21
Dunnock, 6

Earthworm, 64
Elder, 29
Emperor dragonfly, 61
Emperor moth, 63
English oak, 30
Eucalyptus, 25

Fallow deer, 88
Feral pigeon, 8
Field grasshopper, 54
Field maple, 36
Foxglove, 72
Fritillary, 71
Frogbit, 77

Garden slug, 65
Garden snail, 64
Garden spider, 65
Garden tiger moth, 45
Ghost moth, 54
Giant crane fly, 61
Glow worm, 54
Golden eagle, 23
Golden plover, 20
Golden-ringed dragonfly, 60
Goldenrod, 80
Golden samphire, 78
Goldfinch, 4
Gorse, 80
Grass snake, 90
Great crested newt, 91
Greater bindweed, 85
Great spotted woodpecker, 11
Great tit, 5
Great willowherb, 83
Greenfinch, 5
Green lacewing, 45
Green leafhopper, 56
Green shield bug, 51
Green tiger beetle, 62
Green tortoise beetle, 55
Green woodpecker, 11
Grey heron, 19
Grey squirrel, 86

Harebell, 81
Hazel, 28
Heath assassin bug, 62
Heather, 81
Heath speedwell, 80
Hedgehog, 87
Herald moth, 52
Herb Robert, 68
Holly, 29
Holm oak, 42
Honeysuckle, 69
Hornbeam, 32
Horned treehopper, 51
Hornet, 50
Horse chestnut, 24
Horse fly, 50
Houseleek, 67
House martin, 14
House mouse, 87
House sparrow, 8
Hoverfly, 47

Ivy-leaved toadflax, 67

Jackdaw, 13
Jay, 10
Juniper, 36

Kestrel, 22
Kingfisher, 19

Lapwing, 21
Larch, 32
Large heath butterfly, 63
Larkspur, 84
Lawson cypress, 27
Lesser celandine, 74
Leyland cypress, 24
Little owl, 17
London plane, 24
Long-eared owl, 16
Long-tailed tit, 12

Magpie, 9
Mallard, 18
Marbled white butterfly, 57
Marsh marigold, 82
Marsh violet, 82
Mayfly, 60
Meadow brown butterfly, 57
Meadowsweet, 82
Meadow thistle, 70
Minnow, 93
Minotaur beetle, 62
Monkey puzzle, 27
Monterey cypress, 43
Monterey pine, 43
Moorhen, 18
Mute swan, 18

Nightingale, 11
Nightjar, 17
Norway maple, 25
Nuthatch, 12

Oil beetle, 57
Osier willow, 39
Oxeye daisy, 71
Oystercatcher, 20

95

Palmate newt, 91
Peach blossom moth, 52
Peacock butterfly, 46
Perch, 92
Peregrine falcon, 22
Pheasant, 14
Pied wagtail, 9
Pike, 93
Pipistrelle bat, 87
Policeman's helmet, 76
Pond skater, 58
Poplar hawk moth, 52
Primrose, 72
Purging buckthorn, 37
Purple emperor butterfly, 53
Purple loosestrife, 77

Rabbit, 86
Ragged Robin, 83
Red admiral butterfly, 47
Red campion, 73
Red clover, 71
Red fox, 86
Red-headed cardinal beetle, 53
Red kite, 23
Red squirrel, 89
Robin, 6
Rosebay willowherb, 66
Rowan, 40

Scots pine, 36
Sea aster, 79

Sea buckthorn, 42
Sessile oak, 40
Short-eared owl, 16
Silver birch, 33
Silver-studded blue butterfly, 63
Sitka spruce, 41
Skylark, 15
Small-leaved lime, 33
Small tortoiseshell butterfly, 44
Small white butterfly, 48
Smooth newt, 90
Snowdrop, 74
Song thrush, 6
Sparrowhawk, 23
Spindle, 37
Stag beetle, 50
Starling, 8
Stinging nettle, 67
St. John's wort, 84
Swallow, 14
Swamp cypress, 38
Sweet chestnut, 31
Swift, 9
Sycamore, 26

Tamarisk, 42
Tawny owl, 17
Tench, 92
Three-spined stickleback, 92
Thrift, 79
Treecreeper, 13

Vapourer moth, 48
Violet ground beetle, 51
Viper's bugloss, 79

Wasp beetle, 53
Water crowfoot, 77
Water measurer, 58
Weasel, 88
Weeping willow, 34
Western hemlock, 41
Whirligig beetle, 59
Whitebeam, 27
White dead-nettle, 69
White poplar, 34
White water-lily, 76
Wild cherry, 33
Wild pansy, 85
Wild service tree, 31
Willow warbler, 10
Wood anemone, 72
Wood woundwort, 73
Wren, 7
Wych elm, 41

Yellow archangel, 74
Yellowhammer, 15
Yellow horned poppy, 78
Yellow pimpernel, 75
Yellow water-lily, 76
Yew, 31

First published in 2024 by Usborne Publishing Limited, 83–85 Saffron Hill, London EC1N 8RT, United Kingdom. usborne.com
Copyright © 2024, 2019 Usborne Publishing Limited. The name Usborne and the Balloon logo are registered trade marks of Usborne Publishing Limited. All rights reserved. No part of this publication may be reproduced, stored in a retrieval system or transmitted in any form or by any means without the prior permission of the publisher. Printed in China. UKE.